Days / Occasion

Days for an Occasion

POEMS 1978 - 2016

Kitrell Andis

Chatter House Press
Indianapolis, Indiana

Days for an Occasion
Poems 1978 - 2016

Copyright© 2016 by Kitrell Andis

Cover photo by Ron Herrell

All rights reserved.

Except for brief quotations embodied in critical articles and reviews in newspapers, magazines, radio or television, no part of this book may be reproduced in any form or by any means electronic, mechanical, or by any information storage and retrieval system without written permission from the publisher.

For information:

Chatter House Press
7915 S Emerson Ave, Ste B303
Indianapolis, IN 46237

chatterhousepress.com

ISBN: 978-1-937793-36-4
Library of Congress Control Number: 2016942331

Dedication

for Ron Wray
& for John Clark

Acknowledgements

The author would like to thank the following publications in which some of these poems have or will soon appear:

Atom Mind, Happy Kitty, Nuvo Newsweekly, pLopLop, Primer and *So It Goes.*

The author also wishes to thank, in memoriam, Fielding Dawson for getting him over his fear of Russian vodka and Robert Creeley, for doing all the dishes.

POEMS

I Locations
Poem for F. — 3
Preliminary Findings — 5
A Painful Conundrum — 7
Two Poems for Bill — 8
Cartography — 9
Saturday — 10
Propositions — 11
Third & Fourth Propositions — 12
For B. — 13
The Compass — 15

II Hearts Make Fists
Guilty — 19
Dear Chris — 21
Twenty-fifth Street Tableau — 22
Quadna, Weekend — 24
Research — 26
Thursday — 27
Friday — 28
Doubts — 31
Shazam! I Think Therefore I Think — 34
Poem Beginning — 35
Signs of Life — 36
Last Poem for Bill: Adios — 38

POEM	41
POEM	42
DEAR VONDA	43
LONG HAUL	45
SPIRIT OF LIFE	47
29 AUGUST, 6:45 P.M.	48
VOWS	50
NEXT DOOR TRAGEDY	52

III LIKE PARADISE, ONLY DIFFERENT

HOW TO MAKE POEMS	57
HAPPY BIRTHDAY, RICHARD	59
HERE WE GO AGAIN	60
BAD OMEN	61
JOHN BERRYMAN IS DEAD	62
THE MUSE	66
DEAR ALLEN	69
DRESS REHEARSAL	71
AFTER THE READING	72
HIRSUTE HAIKU	74
NEW ORLEANS FEBRUARY, 1997	75
BIG HEART	77
MY FIRST FEMINIST	80
LIKE PARADISE, ONLY DIFFERENT	83

IV AFTER

YAHOO, POETRY	89
FOR ILENE	90
TOO LATE	92
THE CLOTHES SHE WORE	93
WARMING UP	94
MERRY X-MAS MY TIGHTENING LITTLE ASSHOLE	96
BETTER THAN SEX	97
SOME LINES ON PARIS	98
LIAR	99
RED FLAGS	100
BROKEN MIRROR	102

I
LOCATIONS

Poem for F.

I took off work Monday morning
went up to the park on St. Clair to start this poem
quote: I think I am in love
again
the question unwound in the greeting
eyes that pull me across the room
into them
now 2 possibilities spread into 1

and another question
or maybe the same one
can I continue making this poem up?
we did the next afternoon
Saturday
Cosby Lake/St. Paul
the sky open above us
a green knoll rolling gradually down on the shore
a dirt path we followed around
a bridge
a dock, water bobbing it
or later
that night, W. A. Frost & Co., the bar I mean
holding hands
leaning across the table to kiss
talking Van Gogh, Franz Kline & Fielding Dawson

maybe there is something ironical somewhere in all of this
but it isn't strange really that so much of your life can
turn around in a few hours
the mind should be saved for the best questions
right now our lives are taking new shape around the one
in these lines

it extends into a daydream
my curiosity jumps ahead to any number of hopeful possibilities
cities to be explored
a first apartment
the conversations we'll have
and, according to your dream, you come in one day
say, I'm late
now that's life

I am in Schwartz's now, finishing this over beers, wondering
what you are doing
last night my 2nd ex-wife called to read her new poems and
say how happy she is living alone with her daughter
but that she misses my mind
what about the rest of me?
and you are up north talking to an attorney
saying goodbye to your husband
and I wonder what can be said about any of it
at the heart
excitement exists by the recognition of itself elsewhere
5/27/78

Preliminary Findings
(letter to a friend in the hospital)

Brubeck's on loud in the other room
maybe that'll bring me up
        yes I
do remember
how could I forget?
your voice, eyes, hair
the articulation of gestures
—all the particulars I keep among my own
caretaker now for whatever they decide is unhealthy

remember the
face you found in Bill's painting?
or the blue chalk lines jumping off
into the dark in my head?
do they really believe it's that simple
by chemical intrusion from the
real Real
to divide you dividing
you
        till you fit?

it isn't unusual
that I'd talk about it here
to salve where it's bad inside
or simply return to the space around me some sound
—I *am* that romantic
to imagine always
somewhere
a heart lost by the loss of another
inevitable in the balance
but that's not what this talking is
it's the spread of the unit that
interests me
and Reality's got nothing to do with it
that conception's a big white elephant
for which strangely there's a vast market

      and probably
there isn't anything I can do about it
or for you
but find how to be here
—here now
as you must be here now
and maybe, that's everything
and enough
9/6/78

A Painful Conundrum

It's later
and the man wonders
what brought the bird
swooping
to join
him in his living room
(the fading imprint of a wing on glass
dusty feathers perfectly etched).
It has no metaphor for this reality.
Suddenly the air
just stops?
4/22/78

Two Poems for Bill

it's 2:00 a.m.
I listen to Eric Clapton
out of his good heart Bill
gave me a radio
I'm broke and lonely
and he knows it
now I have camaraderie
and my ears are busty

in a dream
in a studio across the park
I am introduced
—presented
a green wig, wreathed to insure peace
and fresh vaginal casts
along her rib cage, the model's nervous
cold drop of sweat
Marcel is of course silent
the poet, from Indiana
Bill says
Oh
replies M. Mutt

Cartography

       on her side
back to me
a mountain slope from shoulder to hip

below
foothills of the spine trace the back as
it narrows

gratefully I've had time to
map this body

what terrain she must be wandering now
a green hillside of dreams
opening like flowers
that other fragrance lingering
on us still
7/12/78

SATURDAY

up
coffee and eggs, a bath before noon

wide
blue space of sky
icy wind stiffening against the back
walking
        down
                the
                        hill
to town
—cigars and liquor
up
brow stinging
fingers numb

pleasant afternoon
slightly drunk
tape record poems, letters, sounds
—nap

out tonight
—later
friends, drinks, talk
—late, late
home stumbling
one last drink
a cigarette

PROPOSITIONS

I do not come to you as
an idea
but arrive at one is us
—and how more beautifully to

I am not other than anything
objects, the senses, thoughts
all simply here

can this be useful to me?
yes, endlessly

two,
the story's not the value
it is less interesting what finally happens
than how
and that it does

Third & Fourth Propositions

language is a spatial dimension
may be a metaphor
and useable
but then that's a matter of timing

IS:
a verb overwhelmed by activity
and certainly a BIG PROJECT

For B.

who would have thot
who would?
eyes—
I had forgotten how green sometimes
hands,
legs, the face
(engaged this minute in activity somewhere)

memories filling all that space
4 years come suddenly to spread here
—there
to go back
to have gone

the city somehow new
you
the bar
Sinatra loud, beer, talk of everything
end of day
Xmas-shopping crowds
a truck in an alley to piss behind
metal cold against bare hands
who would have thot
who would?
the body is all that information
and what do with the affection?
kissing
hand on cheek, fumbling
or inside you then

now
your letter wanting *Who am I? Please translate*
how say it?
it *was* romantic
you *were*
held in a syntax with the past
—I also wanting to feel that way
but we can become those objects
ourselves
quote: not
memories, but a memory of memories
and it is all the difference

The Compass
(A Note for Ron Wray & Ed Dorn—Indianapolis, 11/8/77)

I don't know if we were the real people there
or not
we rode an old white Nova
perverse in its inclination to carry us always into a new
complication
well, that's style anyway
and that day
each time
Ron signaled left
the arbitrary fell into the relative
I mean we *honked* those right angles
and Ed in the back rolled a fat one
passed it around in a gesture to that combination
       and the bar, too
Hollywood leaning garishly in thru a big screen
the colors became confused and everybody's
face turned green
and the pinball machines along the
wall crossed their circuits for quarters
going, I think, quite mad
and the patrons simplified everything down to requests for
more change

Ed chuckled softly——another?
let's
we were composed and we knew it
we had a reference
and all the time it would take to explore
the sound of that direction

II
HEARTS MAKE FISTS

GUILTY

35 years ago
her little cunt was
as bald as my head
is now.
35 years,
goddamn. I can
picture it like
yesterday.
It only cost me
the loan of a Boy Scout hatchet
I'd borrowed myself
from a friend.
She was a new girl,
moved in just up the street.
She pulled down her panties
and lifted her dress
there in the weeds by the railroad tracks.
Later, she lost the fucking hatchet
in the creek. My friend bawled
how his ma would skin him alive
when I told him.
I said, Fuck that.
I saw her pussy, man.
The next week she offered
one of her old man's Salems
to see my little pencil.

Then we tried to do it
there on the bank by the creek
among weeds, hobo shit and broken wine bottles
while some of the guys watched
from the trestle.
35 years.
I wonder, what's the statute of limitations
on childhood curiosity,
sitting here
in my suburban ranch home
—my minister neighbor,
the cop on the next block?
Maybe I could get arrested
for just writing this poem.
35 years now
since the adrenaline rumble and clank
of a sudden old freight
or the smell of weeds and
shit and dank creek water.
35 years
since that first raw wonder.

Dear Chris

Someday
sooner or later
everybody gets the blues
I guess.
Like in a cartoon,
a safe drops from a 10th floor window
smashing thru
& breaks your heart.
Okay,
I'm not telling you anything.
Last night your ex called,
came over. Tonight
her sister calls, asking can you come to dinner
on Thursday.
Now you're at the bar—looking
for what?
And I sit here watching
Harry-O,
typing, wondering.
No, I'm not going to say,
"You do this to yourself,"
       or
"My God,
don't things ever change?"
As Harry said,
"Sometimes just being alive
is lonely enough."

Twenty-fifth Street Tableau

Summer days
thicken with noises of transition
      USED BOOKS : SALE : CHEAP
An ear-phoned young black kid
bobs by, 12 or 13, yells
"'Ey, baby. *'Ey!*"
to every woman passing

  & cars nose carefully, honking
out of the alley
avoiding a herd of bicycles, 10-speeds
(a blur of shining spokes & bare
legs) *swish* past
propelled by a back-pack faith
in the future
Time is *theirs*, they *own* it
not as measurement, but as nature
a law
it stretches like so many well-lit tunnels
out before them, these youths
as straight & as uncomplicated
as imaginary lines can be

down the alley
5 or 6 black men, talking
standing behind a crumbling apartment
building
a kid tosses a can
to the cracked blue bottom
of a long-ago emptied pool   a jam box
blares & no
reason here to measure the empty afternoon
they wait   & waiting, the day passes
          then
at midnight
a cruiser's spotlight fingers the cars
in the dark parking lot
a young cop probing boredom
longing to be engaged

Quadna, Weekend

Hill City,
the resort (townhouse).
Friends, the
long weekend. A
good time.

The sky,
some of it blue.
A wind shaking leaves
on trees standing against
it &
a green hill
sloping down to
the choppy water. No
canoes today.

Take a walk. Yes.

Corny Polka
band in the corny cocktail
lounge.
Out of place except
with each other.

Mosquitoes &
the final edge of
dusk—
a blue line of daylight
on the other side of a
dark lake.

Something, yes. And
certain.

Smoke. Beer.
Turn the lights on.
Evening again.

Research
—for Bob Banta

neon: diner neon: plate
glass neon: people neon:
fender/
Kerouac
Breton-blue eyed in
faded snapshot
dissolving into red brick / you
follow

Thursday

There is a sky,
low,
gray this morning
& fog, starting to lift
—leaves are falling.

The streets
wet, reflect the urgency of
headlights
—cars, people intently in them,
buildings & trees, blocks
—go by
& for a moment
it *is* simple:
pictures,
they are here.

Friday

A car with a bad muffler drives
past the house—
take notes: Her
laughter sounds nervous.
Does she want
acceptance?

It's after midnight, I'm
tired, drained.

I remember her painting:
her father,
pious but weak, holding
his Mama
whom he loves   unlike
his wife, of whom he is afraid,
who hands out his
allowance,
          whom he obeys.

All week I've wasted days.
I read
from a book in the library
to pass the time—
("Time destroys fixed ideas...")
sunlight reflecting
glare from the polished table top
fighting with my concentration

What does that mean?

She is painting her
autobiography—
father, mother   her
brother & sister
      herself,
then kids.
Looking for an emotion of relief
(I guess) under
all the anger & emptiness
—Mother
taught her how to deal with
fear.

What did we ever give
one another
that might hold us here?

I wonder.
The idea
of family disturbs
me—
I could not play to it,
nor become a part of
her autobiography

& she
—I have a photograph of her
smile,
remember her big breasts
& belly
slim paper-white legs—
images she wants to share
with others
& which even now
begin to trail away
from me.

How should it end?
I can imagine
the film:
(*closeup*)
his face in the bus window   (*tracking*)   her
back walking away &
then (*medium*)
exhaust behind the
bus pulling out
                but—

Doubts

It can't really be that simple,
but then again it
        is
a matter of words,
they make up the worlds
we walk into.
It's Wednesday
and only September,
but I can feel winter coming.
That much I know.

And it was like that—
like in a movie.
He was, as they say,
taken by love
                again.
One heart
traded in hope and pain
for another—
and
as he saw her, threw his lonely eyes at her,
they recognized each other
—chose—
it went
            —fast.

Afterward
he wondered
had she seen the doors in his eyes close?
A familiar feeling
of dread floated to the surface.

Why is it so cloudy
all of a sudden?
That's what I want to know.
I tried to make a list
the other night:
WHAT I WANT TO BELIEVE IN
(a) the importance of friendship (b) the value of speaking what we don't already know (c) that something can somehow exist outside time

Do you really love me?
Everybody asks everybody that question,
which is not to say it doesn't count.
Sometimes he looks at her dead husband's safety helmet
over the fireplace;
it feels like something emptying very fast inside.
You're bringing that uncertainty back
into my life, she says. I don't like it.
It frightens me.
He looks at her, not knowing
what to say. Has she
seen those doors in his eyes close?

        Well—
luck can be as good as anything else.
I woke up this morning, I was alive,
I didn't have to think about it.
Another list comes to
mind, WHAT I KNOW
(a) the light in the sky is changing (b) life continues begging the response: I don't know (c) there are moments when the skin of one heart slips along the skin of another that hold us beyond all other things.

He looks at a photo of her smiling face
on his wall. Is it giving, open? Did she choose?
        And something
in him fills up. It
is not that
        doubt
lies like a mouth
under everything,
but that somehow it
lends value.
The sky is getting gray, scudding.
I want to watch my feet now,
one in front of the other,
and get it right.

Shazam! I Think Therefore I Think
(Sometime B.C.)

Listen:
it's a secret
don't tell anyone.

She/he awoke
the glitter of first
life in his/her eyes
—dazed
surprised.

Don't tell the
elephants
drunk on roots in
the fields.
Nor the goddamned
monkeys
giving each other
the finger
holding their testicles
& their young.

It's like a
miracle. Everyone's
been waiting so long.
The look in her/his
eyes, like a sound:
a bomb
or a plague
or maybe a song.

Poem Beginning

a
beginning:
who
owns
this
me
my
name
this
image
caught
by
light
in
the
mirror
today
this
week

43
yrs
hair
bald
genes
wife
friends
breath
these
words
or
how
you
read
them
every
end
is

Signs of Life
—for Vonda

Who, me?
        yes,
you, us—
that space, which
is not a space,
that we are

it is morning, early
a young girl walks
by the pool, her heels clicking
on the cement apron
you are asleep, but
I can
see your eyes
open as you awaken
and on the pillow, your
lovely and only face,
which I touch with my mind,
as you climb back into yourself,
and you realize who you are

only words
and more is the pity
for what is real
                really?
that woman on the balcony
of another apartment
calling to her daughter by the pool?
a squirrel's chittering bark
at our cat in the window?

later,
this afternoon or tonight,
tomorrow evening,
your fingers entwine with mine
and our tongues touch
we hold each other,
I ease inside you

it is a time, which is not time,
but a moment
in which there is no death,
no degradation,
nowhere will there be the need for relief

later still,
a woman on the balcony of another
apartment calls out
and our cat chitters back
from the window
but they are not only words now

the sky *is* blue, the leaves *are* green
you and I do not have to say
anything
and we know it,
which is not knowing,
but recognition
they are the signs by which
we wed

Last Poem for Bill: Adios

Bruce just sent a photo I'd been
asking for
of Luke the Drifter
& which I'm going to come see again
for myself this summer
& I've still got those
two small pieces
& once in awhile your son
writes or calls
                but now
sitting here writing this
I have to look
back   I don't want to wax nostalgic
about the good old days
& maybe I don't even have to make sense
you got a body, don'tcha
Bruce said on Houston Street
that morning when I complained I didn't
know how to look at your work
later I told Walt I had become
an object, too
or maybe it was earlier
fuck, I don't remember
anymore

my body has changed, is
changing, tho not as much
as yours   anyway, I'm not going
in reverse yet
I couldn't come in May
but I heard about the service
& scattering your ashes
on the grounds at Hillsdale
—John & Bruce & Jim
Sandy & Jack
my wife & I drove out
in June
I was reading Artuad
—what he said about Van Gogh, you
know
          pure violence
to make something
anything
to make it all new
again
in a world where people only
want the same, everything the same
I guess I wanted to touch base
one last time
but I got drunk in a restaurant in Woodstock
& made an ass of myself
now I'm tired of grief

it's 5 a.m. & I just want to
make some sense, say something
Bruce said
you showed him a painting of Cezanne's
pointing to a door in it
saying that was his way out
tho he had the feeling you were talking
about yourself
what can I say?
okay, it was no big surprise
& now you're caught in the past tense
forever   I think about
the weight of solid objects
sound, too
& bodies in motion
everything happening faster & faster
        pure violence
I do it, too
I don't know if it's any good, like O'Hara
said, I just know that I do it
& when I look at the photo of Luke
or the stamped metal piece on my wall
I know I got it
I told Bruce
an I for an eye
I get it

Poem

Dawn
small statement
in green digital
numerals: 5:51 a.m.

and
in the light
spreading
on the gray carpet

tho, no
I can't see
the sky
I know, and I know
again

Poem

overcome
with boredom I
sit down to write is
this the real part of reality
something has to be delicately fold
back the words look inside
turn them all around
start again and
emocrevo

Dear Vonda

It does not help
now
to say this
pain in you shall pass,
become then
(a warm place in
heart's memory)

I know,
I know

But as Ed
or Tuli
or Ted or somebody
said, quote:
When someone dies...
they pass from your outside life
to your inside
& I
said: Well,
that's how much love is

"born of
the prostate,
born of the
flashes of the
vulva"
released into light
& space,
caught by time
to touch   to feel
to think &
to wonder
we "live at the mansion of earth
for eighty years in the warmth"
then gone,
passing to someone else's
inside life

& these words now
to touch you, hold you
as you hold your pain
till it passes

Long Haul
—for Tim Slongo

Flipping thru a book of poems with my friend
I run a finger down:

> "Slowly in the swamps unfold
> great yellow petals of a
> savage thing..."

which he kind of liked
& then on to another
        something about being bald
(I am)
which he didn't
so much

in the end we agreed
everyday poems are o.k.
too

o joy of walking down the street
or getting a drink of water
squinting at a blazing sun
staring at a crack
in the cement
without any big ideas
raising static on the receiver

it's been a long haul
since that first question
(what's that?)
opened in the swamp
        maybe our gift
      to ask
              in wonder
the petals of our thots
wet with dew

Spirit of Life

From my hand   fingertips
to chapped lips
touch breath
or simply take another drag
lost in thot
back to when life
was new
& blossomed time
the future stretched out
dumb as emptiness
clip-clop it trotted
then ran
biography flashing by
to here, now
& looks ahead, knowing
someday
it all comes crashing down
but this ain't no sentence
no tiny black hole at the end
Period

29 August, 6:45 p.m.

At my wobbly table
on the patio
I watch my cat
watching me
thru the glass door.
I hear the sizzle of the barbecue.

It's all so peaceful
so serene.

Above us
the evening cries of birds
darting
        diving
against a whitening sky
followed by a honking V of geese
getting smart
getting the hell out.
The cat's mouth isn't
even watering,
it's so peaceful.

I'm caught by my reflection in
the glass
like a prisoner of the subdivision:
20 pounds overweight
bags under my eyes
smoking my cigar
drink in hand.

I'm grilling steaks
from cows
someone else killed
somewhere far away.
And my cat
will eat her tuna from a can
here, hundreds of miles from the sea
where it was caught.

Yes, it's peaceful here.
And my cat & me
waiting on our dinners
waiting on our tumors
kill 15 minutes
with a little
poetry.

Vows

It's September
almost fall
again   rain
& cold
& winter
         coming

turning
we re-
member
put back together
the music

early frost
Pop predicts
& we watch each
other & friends
a jumpy video
of the ceremony
making ourselves
a life
our faces say
it all
& long
for more

grief, too
the other fine
edge   we
buried
our dead   holding
cold hands
waiting
for spring

& it will
come again
to the
music
we've learned
how
to listen
we   do

Next Door Tragedy

What have we here?   Well
there was Jessie
who lived across the alley
who waited one night
for his wife to come home
from her sister's
and who sat in his recliner
with his 12 gauge
waiting. He was
my neighbor
tho not very neighborly
and he sat in his LA-Z-BOY
waiting for his wife Tristessa
who called herself Teresa
who was neighborly without being
familiar
who wanted her husband Jessie
to quit putting in 16-hour days
now that their 9 kids were all grown
and out of the house
and who had no idea
what a break she gave herself
when her sister invited her to stay
for pizza and a new movie on HBO
and she said, Okay

while Jessie, who'd come home early
sat waiting
cradling his oily double-barrel
and drinking almost a quart of cheap bourbon
tho he never drank
except earlier that day
when he'd stopped by the Legion
for happy hour and sat by himself
talking to no one
till he left, saying suddenly
out of nowhere: Fuck it, I'll kill her
to everyone or to himself or to no one at all
who then stopped at the liquor mart
and went home and waited.

What we have here is a story
or the beginning of one.
We'd need plot, for causation
and background for motivation
and a new love interest for Teresa
for a little heart twist
not a boyfriend exactly instead of her sister
but a concerned male friend
—a priest in religious crisis, or a doctor who thinks Jessie has
a brain tumor he can cure.

Hollywood might buy it
or maybe Ted Turner.
Sure. I an see Jane Fonda
paint on her face
half Mexican, half white
shoot mostly interiors, low light.
But this isn't Atlanta or Hollywood.
And the ending won't work for them.
I can hear it now
as they shake their heads. No way.
Because I can't answer why
Jessie finally got tired
of waiting, bowed his head
and tripped both triggers.
Hollywood could answer that
but this is only next door
across the alley
where Jessie waited until he got tired.
And I have no idea
what went thru his mind
when he pressed both thumbs down
except lead.

III
Like Paradise, Only Different

How to Make Poems

Dear Jerry,
start like this:
nothing at all in
mind, except maybe
your best friend's ear
—no subject,
no form,
& for God's sake
no ax to grind.
Now that's rhyme
& it's o.k.
but not necessary.
Poetry is EVERYWHERE.
To start,
        start here—
a fart under the blankets
at 3:00 a.m.,
your girlfriend mumbling
in bad breath.
        Or that limping,
mutt-yellow dog you saw
cause a head-on collision,
killing 2,
& don't forget
how you laughed (just
before)
as the dog danced
on a patch of ice,

or the dog's mournful cry,
digging into
your heart,
the sound of bone
snapping,
& how it hunkered,
snarling, gnashing
when you tried
to help it.
                      And,
of course,
don't forget
how your girlfriend
sat up
in her sleep, suddenly
wincing at the smell
of your fart
& cursed you,
calling you by
your best friend's
name.

Happy Birthday, Richard

It's funny
I first read *Trout Fishing*
21 years ago—
half my life ago.
This morning
when my wife woke me
she whispered, "Happy Birthday."
Then we made love
and I thot of Christopher Columbus
taking off his shoes.
I don't know why
but I remembered it was your birthday, too.
Tonight she baked a cake
and I blew the candles
out. But it felt lonely.
I imagined the house in Bolinas
where they found you
and thot I heard the sound
of a beautiful car parked only
being hot-wired.

Here We Go Again

Ezra Pound said
that to publish a book of poems
in the United States of America
was like dropping a rose petal
into the Grand Canyon
hoping to hear
an echo.
Or so
a young poet told me.
I started to say—
but he cut me off.
"Listen:
what was that?"

Bad Omen

watching Yul B.
posthumously on TV
flex his big muscles
flex his big tumors
talk about dying
of lung cancer

I stub one out
light another
wonder if it's a bad omen
my being bald

John Berryman is Dead

Etheridge stopped the car
near the end of the bridge
on Washington Avenue,
below yellow rectangles in campus windows.
It was late,
so there wasn't much traffic.
Nobody even started honking
till we got out
and carried our beers over to the railing.
"Right here," he told me.
"He got out of his cab
waved to someone
and over he went."
"Who?" I asked.
"What?"
"Who'd he wave to?"
Etheridge scratched the scar on his chin
and started to grin.
"Shit, man, you got no respect."
"Not for death," I told him.
Back in the car
we drove on in silence
drinking our beers.
"So, what? You think poetry
did him in?" I finally asked.
Etheridge looked over at me,
one eyebrow going up.

"Kit, you not makin' any sense
at all. Poetry brings you life,
not death. Was white-boy angst
did him in. No offense."
It was my turn to lift an eyebrow
at that crack
so pregnant with irony.
Again he grinned.
I have thought of this often
over the years—
in Philly, where I got him a gig at a jazz club
& he no-showed,
in Memphis, in his house
with no electricity or gas,
no wife, no kids, filled with abandoned
baby cribs—on
and on.
It was like a center of gravity
for a dozen years
of conversations—driving him to a bank
or a methadone clinic
or detox
or a liquor store.
"*White-boy angst*?" I'd ask. "Come on, man."
He'd shake his large head.
"Kit, just cause you ain't no tight-ass
don't mean it's not in your blood."
And he'd grin.

He was at some university
signing books
the last time I saw him.
He jumped up from the table
and I saw those big teeth
as he held me. "Hey, where you been?"
We gossiped—so and so, this and that.
He lit a Pall Mall, shook one out for me.
"I got lung cancer," he said. "Inoperable.
Six months they're saying."
He wasn't asking for anything.
Just telling me.
I didn't know what to say. I said,
"That's rough."
He sat back down
and started signing more books.
Then he remembered, "Hey, I saw one of your poems
in—" and he named the magazine.
"Kit, you did good, man,
you did good."
Then I remembered. "Etheridge,
you know that night on the bridge?
You were right. You were right
about everything."
Of course he grinned, "Man,
you're so full of shit. You know it,
too."

I didn't go to the big shindig
they threw, just before he died.
I didn't want to see him all skinny,
all skull.
I still don't. I want to see him
leaning over the rail of the bridge,
a cigarette in one hand, a beer
in the other,
car horns honking,
people giving us the finger,
and Etheridge taking his sweet time,
considering the irony.

The Muse

She's the oldest whore in the world
the first whore
she was in the caves
in France
shakin' her wet
hairy thing
getting those bison & deer
up onto damp, torch-lit walls
in Greece she
crossed gender
had big biceps
& eight hard inches
in Rome
she wore see-thru silk
trailing along marble halls
in the Renaissance
there was a red velvet cape
& a funny hat
in drag as the Pope
in Nineteenth Century Paris
she crossed again

o, she smoked opium in
studios, slugged down
absinthe in left bank cafés
gave out teasing little come-on looks
but when you got her back against
the wall on the rue Moderne
fumbling under her skirts
you found she was built like
a Swiss clock
beneath all that cotton & lace
all you touched was metal
slippery with oil
& fine-tuned, tiny moving parts

                  Now, this isn't a
sexually political take   the Muse
can accommodate you
whatever your gender or persuasion
o.k.   but for me
she's in a white skirt
bare legs
& a low-cut black top
disappearing down a dark hall
& out the back, under a red-lighted EXIT sign
she is an envelopment of perfume
words whispered: "Come on, baby, hurry, I'm so wet"
she is a hangover the next morning
and no money left

she is a divorce from your wife
who knows you're fooling around
she is a look of disgust on your neighbors'
& co-workers' faces
she is bankruptcy & jail
& doing without what everyone else wants
& you don't need
but she is a possibility
she is a world to create
she is the machine & the paper
& words ruining white space
her wet dark hole
is the mouth of a tunnel
you enter willingly
hungrily
crawling on your hands & knees
knowing you might die
but she is the opposite of death

So keep the Muse alive
and on her back where she belongs

Dear Allen

From my friend
a phone call to tell me
you've been diagnosed
with the worst news
& from TV next day
that you're gone
from heart's memory a teen-aged
bedroom wall of photos
& books of poems
from baseball-broken tooth
& funny black-rimmed glasses
from first touch of red-haired
pubis in hometown movie theatre
from magical
secret writings that told
the truth
from jacking off
against Father's angry
What the hell're you doing?
from novels by Jack & Bill
& letters from Neal
from heads clubbed in Chicago
from boot camp
from brains blown out
in Southeast Asia

from letters to the Pentagon
trying to save us all
from a mantra
from an empty mind
from a dozen storm-wrecked
loves
from 30 years of dope & booze
from green youth to middle age
from fear & trembling to glimmers
of peace
from longing for other
to love of self
from shameful desire
to candid speech
from 4 decades of bardic
song
a sudden silence
4/12/97

Dress Rehearsal

At a little past noon
—a minute or two
before the bus was to arrive—
I burst thru the glass door
into the 7-Eleven
digging down into my backpack
feeling around for my day-late video.
The teenaged cashier
stumbled back
a shit-scared look on her face
throwing her hands
in the air.

After the Reading

She played the violin,
she told me.
"Oh, yeah?" I said.
We were at the bar,
I signed her book.
"I don't know how
anyone can live without
art."
She was a big woman
under a loose summer dress.
She put her hand on my arm.
"I really like your work,"
she went on.
"Oh, yeah?"
"You know that one,
the one about the little gir's
pussy?"
"Uh-huh."
"It's my favorite."
We hung there in the moment,
our eyes moving up
and down.
Then her elbow slipped drunkenly off the bar
and she had to catch herself.
I smiled.
It was a good sign.

But I knew
I should have paid more attention to
that earlier part
where she said, "I play violin."
All the way back to her place
I had to listen to how that violin
had saved her
when her marriage was turning to shit,
how art had given her a new life.
She heaved a sigh
and I glanced at those tits moving her her dress,
but I began to wonder
if it was going to be worth it.
We ended up on her living room carpet,
stripping and pawing
and grunting.
"I've never made love to
another artist," she said.
"I'm no artist," I told her.
"Art is just another lie."
But I had my thumb in her ass
by now,
and she didn't object.
The violinist
is the only woman I know
who farts every time she comes
—of course, I had my thumb
out of her ass by then.

Afterward,
sharing a cigarette,
she said she thought two people making love
was like a beautiful concerto.
I thought it sounded
more like a busted kazoo.

Hirsute Haiku

O Lon Chaney Jr
hair is growing on your palms
what the hell have you been doing?

New Orleans February, 1997

Dan sends photos
from New Orleans
he & Mike
Deborah & David
& me
partying
roaming bookstores
bars
& porno shops
no streetcars
in the Quarter
only a bus
named "Desire"
after the projects
where death toll
rises &
O, how tell the truth
about anything
everyone lives
in secret
even from themselves
go to gallery
meet Jewish woman
long red talons
I try to imagine
ripping my back
alas, paintings
disappointing

I long for hot tub
too dirty, Mike
says
I long for oysters
they kill alcoholics
Dan says
I long for fame
& success
ugh, everyone says
I long for love
for ecstasy
for desire
but it's only a bus ride
to death
I end up lonely
in the claw-foot bath tub
nodding & jacking
off   I end
up in a cab to
the airport
I end up on a plane
coming home
I end up with
only one thing

Big Heart

Just like that
sometimes it happens
sparks
under your belly
and your imagination
gets out of hand
in your mind's eye
you try to picture
what's under her dress
a blonde, a brunette
or maybe a redhead, Christ
yeah, you know
how to do it
next thing
you're in bed
trying to unhook a bra
there's a hand
down the front of
your pants
the thud of dropping beers
on the carpet
and the world disappears
for a while

then
you're talking to a judge
or jp
and a new
landlord or realtor
with that special smile
a job comes along
that you can live
with, you think
you learn to watch
how much you drink
then a squalling brat
or maybe an ex-lover
comes like a ghost
to lie between you
and you don't like
each other's friends
every day you start looking
older in the mirror
you wonder how
it all ends
      —well,
you die
or she does
or a deputy knocks on
your door
envelope in hand
a letter from the court
telling you, politely
GET THE FUCK OUT!

or you make amends
watch each other
get even older
sooner or later
you end up
looking at a grave
or at the sky
or somewhere
asking what it all
means
the grave and the sky
have nothing to say
but we have history
institutions
and bodies of knowledge
and lore
to tell you
with some nice metaphor
how you're just human
it's your heart
leads you to these things

My First Feminist

Suzi
        was her name
"Crazy Suzi"
they called her—
guys in the bars
        "tricks"
she called them
or "suckers"
to be led around
by their little heads

San Juan, 1969
no pun intended
Suzi worked the bars
on Calle Luna—
Club Paradise
& others
mostly American boy sailors
& middle-aged Puerto Rican men
fucky sucky—
15 bucks for
a grunt &
a little shiver from heaven
I don't know why
but somehow we were friends
her night ended around 2 a.m.
& if I was in town
she'd buy a chicken

I'd get the bread & wine
we'd split the 7 bucks for a room
she taught me PR Spanish
at least enough to get by
& a little about how to live on the street
mostly we just talked
she thot my jokes were funny

Suzi was too smart & too
tough for any pimp
one night I saw her negotiate
with a 6 inch heel
a bad debt from some trick
who lay on the floor
bleeding
from a hole in his cheek

& then
less than a month
before I left
I stood in a hotel lobby
holding Suzi's purse
while she walked back to a bar
for her drink—
maybe a thousand or so
of her hard-earned green dollars
in my hand

it was a moment of truth, as they
say   I thot
about the guy with the hole
in his cheek, felt my sphincter tighten
I thot about friendship
what did it mean

the weekend before I left
I had to search the bars of Old San Juan
finally found her in a restroom for *Caballeros*
slumped against the toilet paper dispenser
on the nod, her rig still in her hand
"Angel," she said
when I picked her up   a bad omen?
flying home I thot
about all the hard predators on her street
& in her heart
wondering how much longer she could make it last

Like Paradise, Only Different

Little boys and girls
from broken homes
are splashing in the pool
all around me.
It's late July
and hot
and I'm trying to cure my hangover
before I go to work.

The pool is in an apartment complex
where a friend lives.
He and I did a poetry reading
out of town last night.
We just pulled in a half hour ago
tired and shaky
and my friend said, "Let's
take a dip."

I ease away from the boys and girls
kicking into a breast-stroke
and haul my tired ass up over the side.
I towel myself next to my aluminum
and plastic chair
light a soggy 100 and take a sip
of warm beer.

"That town we were in last night
used to have a nude beach," I say.
"An old girlfriend took me there
after a poetry festival
oh, ten—twelve years ago." My
friend doesn't answer.
"Shoulda seen it, man. Tits and ass
everywhere. Couples slippin' off with
their towels to fuck in the bushes
like nothin' at all.
Like paradise.

My friend doesn't answer.
He's staring hard into space.
I put my glasses on and squint in
the direction he's looking.
3 chicks at a table
talking and drinking.
"All right," I say.
My friend nods. "Ex-stripper
single moms."

They are tattooed
pierced
in their early 30s
and a little buzzed from their
morning wine. Their kids
are all squealing
jumping in and out of the pool.

Now, I can't tell you why
women do it
but guys write poetry for pussy.
It's as simple as that.
Unfortunately, fucking for poetry
is no longer hip etiquette.
A little polite applause
is about all you're going to get.
That's all my friend and I got last night
anyway. Plus, of course,
our hangovers.

Opening my 2nd warm can
I see a muscle-bound young guy coming in
maybe late 20s
carrying his sun block
a towel
a bottle of wine
and on his shoulder
a foot-long lizard.
"Jesus!" My friend rolls his eyes.
"How corny can you get?"

But in a New York second
all the little boys and girls
from broken homes
are swarming the young guy's table
to get a better look.

And pretty soon one of the ex-stripper
single moms picks up her drink
tosses her hair
and joins the kids.
Leaning over the young guy's big shoulder
to pet his lizard
the ex-stripper's right tit
pops out of her bikini.
The lizard's eyes slide around
looking at the tit as if trying to decide
if it's something to eat.
The ex-stripper laughs
tosses her hair
and scoops her tit
back into her top
while the muscle-bound young guy
starts to grin.

My friend and I look at each other
then back at the young guy's table.
And like it or not
we have to admit
poetry has failed us
or we have failed poetry.
The warm beer in my stomach
starts burbling
trying to come back up.
"You okay?" my friend asks.
"What?"
"You look a little green."

IV
After

Yahoo, Poetry

Comes along
a silver-hooved
many-legged thot
I ride
into the back rooms
of the mind:
a song.

For Ilene

Coffee
the tobacco you bought—rolled
smoked now
           /in, out
           curling away.
Mostly waiting the
time out
—for you
to be here, for
tomorrow
or happiness
(any possibility to make
one want to go on).

"It's the idea,
or the piece as ideation,"
you like to say.
Okay,
I'll listen,
but it's the sound
itself
(which doesn't last either)
that interests
me—it's as real &
physical
as any other
thing.

& I do look
with eyes.
I have limbs
& skin to go out by
—touching
or words I find to
bring it in.
    Yes,
simply
to come to know
what is here—isn't
the mind insistent.

They collect here,
these things,
to be looked at,
wondered about
—like you,
passing on the street
in black tee shirt, turquoise pants
one hand in the air for waving.

Too Late

This morning
12 hours ago
I had a poem
right here
—trembling on the tips
of my fingers.

That was now,
this is then
4/17/96

The Clothes She Wore

baggy black t-shirts
& jeans
made it hard
to imagine what she would look like
naked
I kept trying to make a picture of her
in mind's eye:
her breasts
hips
pubic mound
thighs
but it kept changing
she seemed shy
the first time I pulled her
to me
her whole body
quaking
like that picture of her in my mind
jarring
out of focus

Warming Up

It came over me
like some chronic disease
I was only eighteen
thick glasses, pimply face
big nose
scribbling in notebooks
or tapping away on my mother's
old Remington
forsaking the beer and the parties
and all that willing pussy
like the fool that I am

my head was full of dreams
of New York glory
and carving out with words
the real truth
sometimes I think I must've been
about the dumbest kid on earth

now, decades later
three wives
and a dozen other women later
thousands of gallons of booze later
hundreds of thousands of cigarettes later
       it's getting later still

and I sit here
at another typewriter
carving out with words
some new hope for truth
and my old lady
is in the other room
watching tv
maybe calculating just how long it's been
and in a minute
when I go to the pantry for another drink
she'll give me that look
and I'll pretend not to see
that beast in the forest
in me
I'll come back to my study
roll in a fresh piece of paper
wonder if I can carve out another poem
all I need is a title
the first line

Merry X-mas My Tightening Little Asshole

We bought ourselves
a shiny new Italian .38
for Christmas.

Her first time out
she put all 5 rounds
in a tight dark group
shaped
like a heart.

Better Than Sex

We brought cold beers
into the bedroom
and made love for 3 or 4 hours
that hot, sticky
summer day.
We lay on damp sheets
holding each other
sweating
drinking Coronas.
Somewhere in there
she asked, "What time is it?"
I looked at my watch on the nightstand,
told her.
She said, "Oh, God.
I gotta go."
I walked out to the mailbox
while she took a shower,
came back in
through the screened door,
and beyond the dog's barking
heard something I didn't recognize.
I thought it must be the radio.
Coming along the hall
I saw her—
her back to me in the bathroom mirror:
she was naked & wet
combing out her hair
       dancing
             & singing.

Some Lines on Paris
—for Deborah

My Paris is only imaginary
as are these lines. You asked for five, I know
don't count them, counting has nothing to do with imagination
It's 4:03 a.m. in our cluttered study
I can't sleep
You have a cold, tossing and turning in bed
coughing
You were upset because the agent tried to put us in a Holiday Inn
which is not how you imagine us in St. Germain des Pres
—in the hotel where you & your sister Cindy stayed
that's what you're thinking
& you have all of those photos, in color
My Paris is eternally in
black & white—Man Ray and his women
or Ernest & Sylvia standing on the walk in front of her shop or
Henry
& Alfred getting drunk and chasing pussy in Place de Clichy
or Jean-Paul B on a corner, a fat Gauloises hanging from his
full lips
You are already en route
planning our days, the meals we'll eat, et cetera

    —& me
    I just want to follow Brassai's steps down into that
foggy night
see where they lead

Liar

It's 10:00 a.m. Saturday & I'm
bored down here
in Madison, IN on the
Ohio (pronounced O-hi-ya) river
& there's workshops going on
that I don't want to participate in
I'm thinkin' of the GF
—what's she doin'?
Sleepin'?
Tho I know if I was there
I'd be wonderin' what's goin' on here
or somewhere.
I'm pretty happy & that's
good.
I'm right in the middle of 2 autobiographies.
Fuck novels!
I'm writing about me
& I know half this shit is just
made up
& I also know I won't tell
anybody, because how can
you explain it to someone who
believes words tell you the truth
even when they're comin' out of people's
mouths?
Really.

Red Flags

Some Wednesday nights,
after our meeting,
Joe & I drive by the place:
BUD'S.
It's an ordinary neighborhood tavern.
But as we drive by
my head turns.
I watch the patrons through the big
plate-glass window: men & women on stools
along the bar,
pool players, dart throwers.
"Thirsty?" Joe asks.
He asks me that almost every time
we drive by.
"No," I tell him.
And he looks at me for a moment,
a little grin pulling at the line of his mouth.
"It was my first time," I tell him. "Well, the first time
I *knew*, anyway."
"Yeah?" he asks.
"Twenty-five years ago. I went in for lunch,
a bowl of chili and a beer. I had about an hour to
kill before delivering a paper on Emily Dickinson.

I remember the waitress.
A redhead with freckles. 'Whataya have, hon'?' I
told her, and a minute later she was back with a cold
longneck. I took the first pull and looked out the big
window, thinking about my professor and the other students.
I could picture
their mouths dropping open
upon hearing my brilliant insights into a Certain
Slant of Light. And then in a quickness that cannot be
measured, the redhead was back. 'That be all, hon'?' She
dropped my check next to my half-eaten bowl of chili.
A dozen empty longnecks stood around the bowl, their red
labels like warning flags. I looked at my watch. "Fuck," I
muttered. The warning flags waved at me. I had driven
through some invisible barrier, full-speed, on a one-lane,
one-way highway."
Joe nods, still grinning. "Yeah,
I know."

Broken Mirror

It's 10:13 a.m. and cold
outside
I am wondering how to get
my energy up
to write this poem
& I can feel these lines
like shards
cut into seeing myself
out there
          —somewhere
ah, romance
ebbing
yes, I'm old
the world is older
seems so
tho it thinks it's young
o Roman
the story has been told
& told again
it is not what
finally happens
but how
& that it does
to lift & so
be lifted
          —excitement

rushing out
to find its reflection
broken
into shards that
fly apart
the universe, they
say
is expanding
& so
I am free
at last
to hold these
pieces
in my bloody
hand

Biography

Kitrell Andis is a poet and fiction writer whose work has been published in newspapers and magazines around the U.S. Since the mid-1970s. His darkly comic novel *Bookstore* charts the downfall of the retail book industry in an hilarious homage to the Olympia Press paperback originals of his youth. Andis's novel *The Summer Ho Chi Minh Died* looks at young men about to be drafted into the Vietnam war.

Andis has taught writing at the Minneapolis College of Art and Design, the Free University of Indianapolis and at Central State Hospital. He has been a newspaper columnist, feature writer, advertising copywriter, and magazine editor, most notably with pLopLop throughout the 1990s, where he also co-edited their chapbook series, publishing over 20 titles in a ten-year period.

Made in the USA
Charleston, SC
27 May 2016